EDGE BOOKS™

PRO SPORTS
by the Numbers

# PRO BASKETBALL
## by the Numbers

by Todd Kortemeier

**Consultant:**
Stew Thornley, NBA Official Scorer and Sports Historian/Author

CAPSTONE PRESS
a capstone imprint

Edge Books are published by Capstone Press, 1710 Roe Crest Drive, North Mankato, Minnesota 56003
www.mycapstone.com

**Library of Congress Cataloging-in-Publication Data**
Cataloging-in-publication information is on file with the Library of Congress.

ISBN 978-1-4914-9058-7 (library binding)
ISBN 978-1-4914-9062-4 (paperback)
ISBN 978-1-4914-9066-2 (ebook PDF)

**Editorial Credits**
Patrick Donnelly, editor
Nikki Farinella, designer and production specialist

**Photo Credits**
AP Images: 4, Ben Margot, 19 (background), Bob Donnan/USA Today Sports Pool, cover (bottom), 1 (foreground), John Swart, 22 (left), Tony Dejak, cover (top); Carl Iwasaki/Sports Illustrated/Getty Images, 22 (right); Newscom: Aaron M. Sprecher/Icon SMI 952, 23 (left), Albert Pena/Cal Sport Media, 8–9 (foreground), 9 (top right), 19 (foreground), Charles Cherney/KRT, 5 (top right), Christopher Szagola/Cal Sport Media, 9 (bottom right), Doug Duran/TNS, 17 (middle bottom), Icon SMI 592/Icon SMI, 23 (right), Icon Sports Media 598/Icon Sports Media, 24, John Fisher/Cal Sport Media, 20, John McDonough/Icon SMI, 17 (top), 28 (left), Kevin Sullivan/MCT, 28 (right), Lee K. Marriner UPI Photo Service, 17, Stephen M. Dowell/TNS, 17 (middle top), TMB/Icon SMI, 18 (foreground); Panacea_Doll/iStockphoto/Thinkstock, 11 (top); Shutterstock Images: cover (right), 11 (bottom), 16, 22, 29, 360b, 26 (left), 26 (right), Alhovik, 9 (hoop), chrupka, 10–11, dean bertoncelj, 5 (top left), designelements, 15, Doug James, 18 (background), Eyes wide, 6–7, gst, 7, J. D. S., 14–15, Nelson Marques, 13 (top), Oleksii Sidorov, 16–17, Pavel Shchegolev, 4–5, 12–13, prophoto14, 21 (background), Torsak Thammachote, 8–9 (background), Ververidis Vasilis, 5 (bottom), Yuliyan Velchev, cover (background), 1 (background), 6–7, 13 (bottom), 21 (bottom), 26–27

**Design Elements**
Red Line Editorial (infographics), Shutterstock Images (perspective background, player silhouettes)

Printed in the United States of America in Mankato, Minnesota
102015   2015CAP

# TABLE OF CONTENTS

The Association ...................................................... 4

The Hardwood .......................................................... 6

The Rock................................................................. 8

The World of Basketball ......................................... 10

Basketball by the 16s ............................................ 12

24 Seconds That Changed the Game.................... 14

The Long and Short of It ...................................... 16

The Rise of Women's Basketball.......................... 18

At the Line/From Downtown.................................. 20

The Dunk Artists.................................................... 22

The Big Dipper Goes for 100................................. 24

The Best of the Best.............................................. 26

Top Performers ...................................................... 28

Glossary................................................................. 30
Read More.............................................................. 31
Critical Thinking Using the Common Core........ 31
Internet Sites......................................................... 31
Index....................................................................... 32

# THE ASSOCIATION

No other professional sport racks up the numbers like basketball. National Basketball Association (NBA) game scores commonly reach triple digits. The greatest players end their careers with tens of thousands of points. Even the heights of the players can be off the charts. Read on to discover some of the amazing numbers the game has to offer.

## Timeline: Milestone Years of Basketball

**1891**
Dr. James Naismith invents the game of basketball.

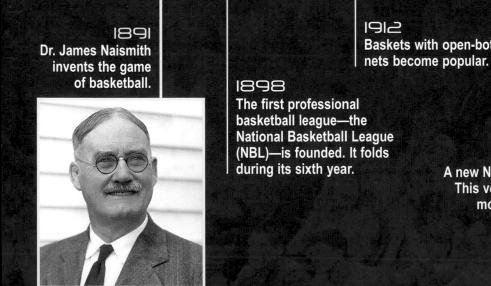

**1898**
The first professional basketball league—the National Basketball League (NBL)—is founded. It folds during its sixth year.

**1912**
Baskets with open-bottom nets become popular.

**1937**
A new NBL is founded. This version is much more successful.

# JOURNEY TO
# 30

The NBA was not always so stable. A lot of teams folded and moved in the early years of the league. It was a long journey as the league established the 30 solid teams it has today.

**1949**
The BAA and NBL merge and call the new league the National Basketball Association.

**1962**
Wilt Chamberlain scores 100 points in a game.

**1998**
Coach Phil Jackson and star guard Michael Jordan win their sixth title with the Chicago Bulls.

**1954**
The 24-second shot clock is invented.

**1979**
The league introduces a 3-point line.

**2008**
The Boston Celtics win their record 17th NBA championship, breaking a 22-year title drought.

**1946**
The Basketball Association of America (BAA) begins play.

**1972**
The Los Angeles Lakers' record 33-game winning streak ends.

# THE HARDWOOD

Every NBA arena is different, but each **court** is the same size. Every measurement on the floor serves an important purpose.

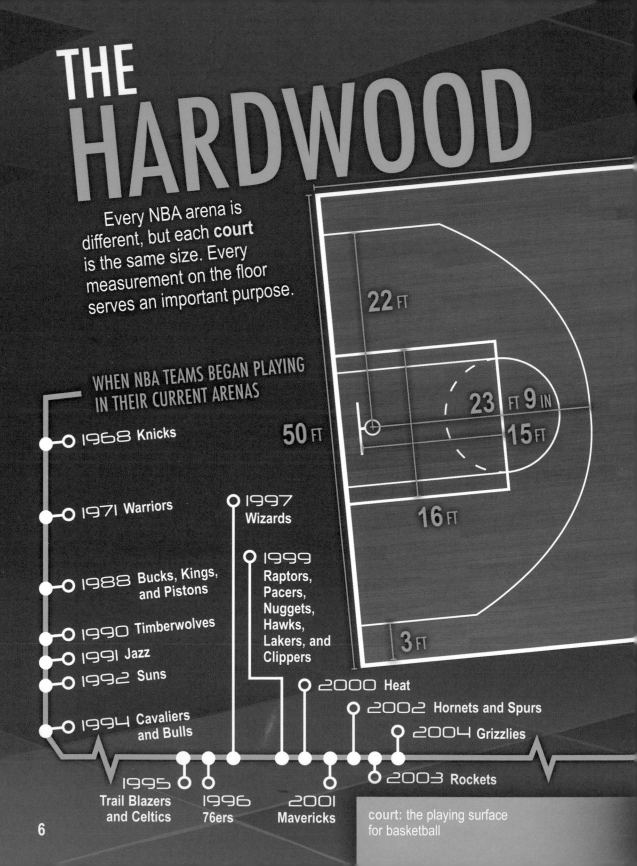

22 FT

23 FT 9 IN

15 FT

50 FT

16 FT

3 FT

## WHEN NBA TEAMS BEGAN PLAYING IN THEIR CURRENT ARENAS

1968 Knicks

1971 Warriors

1988 Bucks, Kings, and Pistons

1990 Timberwolves

1991 Jazz

1992 Suns

1994 Cavaliers and Bulls

1995 Trail Blazers and Celtics

1996 76ers

1997 Wizards

1999 Raptors, Pacers, Nuggets, Hawks, Lakers, and Clippers

2000 Heat

2001 Mavericks

2002 Hornets and Spurs

2003 Rockets

2004 Grizzlies

court: the playing surface for basketball

# Player Positions

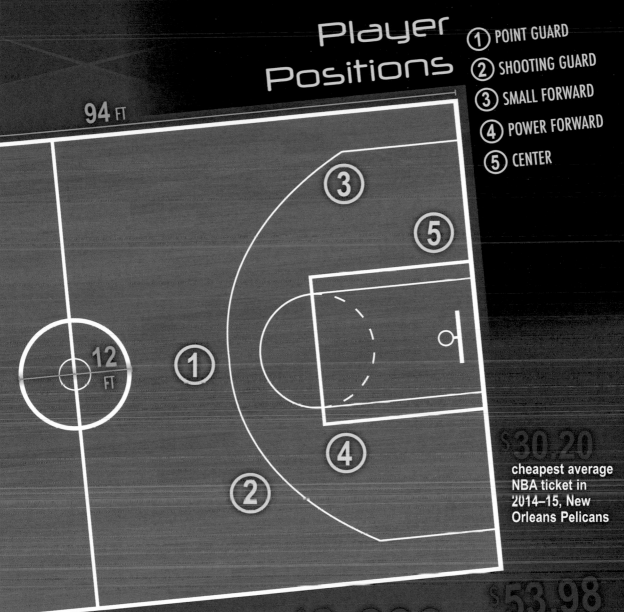

① POINT GUARD
② SHOOTING GUARD
③ SMALL FORWARD
④ POWER FORWARD
⑤ CENTER

94 FT

12 FT

$30.20
cheapest average NBA ticket in 2014–15, New Orleans Pelicans

$53.98
average cost of an NBA ticket in 2014–15

$3,600
price per ticket for a New York Knicks courtside seat

$129.38
average cost of a Knicks ticket in 2014–15, the highest in the NBA

2005
Hornets

2010
Magic

2008
Thunder

2012
Nets

TICKET

# THE ROCK

Dr. James Naismith invented basketball in 1891. In 1894 he asked the Spalding company to design a special ball for his new sport. The first basketball had laces on it; they weren't removed until 1937. The ball we know today has been basically unchanged since 1983. Each ball contains an inflated center covered in nylon. This inner sphere is then covered in rubber, and the leather outer panels are glued on.

**3—4 SQUARE FEET**
amount of leather per ball

**3,200 YARDS**
length of nylon thread used on the ball's inner bladder

**9** number of balls each team provides for pregame warm-ups

**7.5–8.5 POUNDS PER SQUARE INCH**
air pressure of an NBA game ball

**52–56 INCHES**
height a properly inflated ball will bounce when dropped from 6 feet

**29.5–29.75 INCHES**

**72** number of balls issued to each team at the start of the season

**8 PANELS**

OFFICIAL GAME BALL

COMMISSIONER

NBA

**18 IN**

**2** number of balls that can fit in the hoop at the same time

**2 MONTHS** time needed to break in a new ball before game use

**100.5** average number of times Michael Carter-Williams touched the ball per game during the 2014–15 season, which led the NBA

# THE WORLD OF BASKETBALL

Basketball first became popular in the United States, where it was invented. But in time the rest of the world has caught on. It's now one of the world's most popular sports. And players from around the world have a big influence on the NBA.

## 2014-15 NBA Players

22.4% International Players

United States 77.6%

Canada
12

United States
**349**
PLAYERS

Haiti
1

Dominican Republic
2

U.S. Virgin Islands
1

Mexico
1

Jamaica
1

Senegal
1

Venezuela
1

Brazil
7

**215** number of countries with access to NBA games on TV or online

Argentina
3

**1** number of international teams in the NBA, the Toronto Raptors. The Memphis Grizzlies formerly played in Vancouver, Canada.

N
W — E
S

In 1990 the Utah Jazz and Phoenix Suns met in Tokyo, Japan, for the first regular-season NBA game outside of North America. The league has been back to Japan and also visited the United Kingdom and Mexico for regular-season games since then.

## MAP KEY

A. Slovenia: 3
B. Croatia: 2
C. Serbia: 1
D. Greece: 2
E. Macedonia: 1
F. Montenegro: 3
G. Bosnia and Herzegovina: 3
H. Italy: 4
I. Switzerland: 2
J. Spain: 5
K. France: 10
L. United Kingdom: 2
M. Germany: 2
N. Sweden: 2
O. Poland: 1
P. Lithuania: 2
Q. Ukraine: 1
R. Georgia: 1
S. Turkey: 4
T. Israel: 2
U. Democratic Republic of the Congo: 1
V. Republic of the Congo: 1
W. Cameroon: 2
X. Nigeria: 1

Russia
4

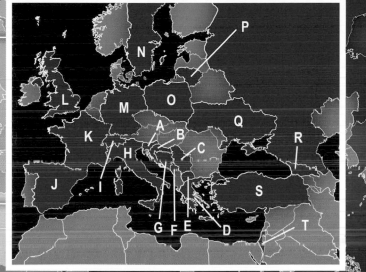

**47**
number of languages in which NBA programming is broadcast

**6**
number of international players in the 2015 All-Star Game

Australia
8

New Zealand
1

# BASKETBALL

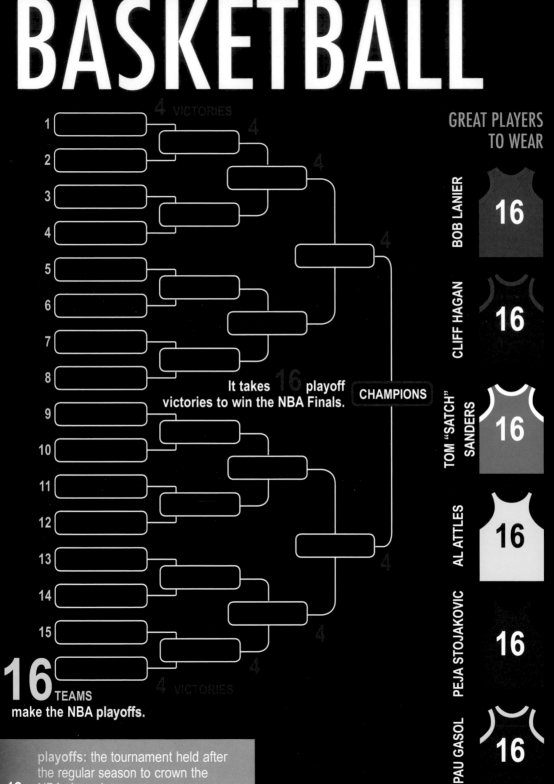

GREAT PLAYERS TO WEAR

4 VICTORIES

4

4

4

4

It takes 16 playoff victories to win the NBA Finals.

CHAMPIONS

4

4

4

4 VICTORIES

16 TEAMS
make the NBA playoffs.

BOB LANIER — 16

CLIFF HAGAN — 16

TOM "SATCH" SANDERS — 16

AL ATTLES — 16

PEJA STOJAKOVIC — 16

PAU GASOL — 16

playoffs: the tournament held after the regular season to crown the NBA champions

12

# BY THE 16s

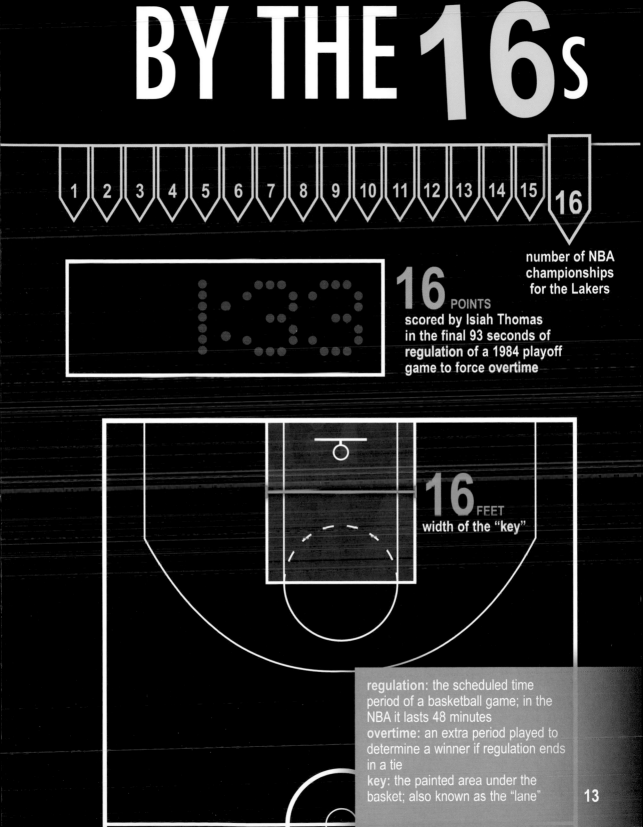

1 2 3 4 5 6 7 8 9 10 11 12 13 14 15 16

number of NBA
championships
for the Lakers

**16** POINTS
scored by Isiah Thomas
in the final 93 seconds of
regulation of a 1984 playoff
game to force overtime

**16** FEET
width of the "key"

**regulation:** the scheduled time
period of a basketball game; in the
NBA it lasts 48 minutes
**overtime:** an extra period played to
determine a winner if regulation ends
in a tie
**key:** the painted area under the
basket; also known as the "lane"

# 24 SECONDS THAT CHANGED THE GAME

The NBA of the 1950s didn't much resemble the high-scoring, high-flying sport we know today. Games were often boring and featured little action. The shot clock helped change that forever. Teams could no longer hold the ball to kill time. They had 24 seconds to shoot. If they didn't get a shot off, the referees blew the whistle and gave the ball to the other team.

Points per team, per game

84.1

82.7

83.7

80    80

72.7

**1953–54: Per-team scoring reaches a five-year low in the season before the shot clock is introduced.**

79.5

67.8

120

100

80

60

1946–47    1947–48    1948–49    1949–50    1950–51    1951–52    1952–53    1953–54

110.6

1957–58:
Every NBA team averages at least 100 points per game.

106.6

118.1

115.3

108.2

99

99.6

93.1

1954–55: In the first season of the shot clock era, the league scoring average increases by nearly 14 points per team. The Boston Celtics become the first team to average 100 points per game for an entire season.

Before the 1954–55 season, teams with less talent could hold the ball and keep it away from their more skilled opponents. Danny Biasone, owner of the Syracuse Nationals, had an idea to fix this problem. Teams should have a set amount of time to get a shot off. But how much time? Biasone used the following formula:

$$\frac{120 \text{ shots/game}}{48 \text{ minutes}} = 24 \text{ seconds}$$

He estimated that in an exciting game, teams combined for approximately 120 shots. He then divided the number of shots into the length of the game—48 minutes, or 2,880 seconds. The result was 24 seconds.

1954–55 | 1955–56 | 1956–57 | 1957–58 | 1958–59 | 1959–60 | 1960–61 | 1961–62

# THE LONG AND SHORT OF IT

Basketball players are known for their height. The average NBA player today is 6 feet 7 inches tall. But some players are anything but average.

Average height of an NBA player

**Feet**

6' 4"

6' 5"

6' 6"

6' 7"

7

6

1950–51  1954–55  1962–63  1980–present

## Shoe Size

SHAQUILLE O'NEAL

LEAGUE AVERAGE

AVERAGE AMERICAN MAN

9

14.81

23

TODAY'S AVERAGE NBA PLAYER IS 3 INCHES TALLER AND 23 POUNDS HEAVIER THAN THE AVERAGE PLAYER IN 1951.

10 feet: height of an NBA hoop

10 ft

9 ft

7 feet 7 inches: Manute Bol (1985–1995, 2,086 career **blocked shots**)

6 feet 8: LeBron James (2003–, 4-time NBA Most Valuable Player)

6 feet 7: average height of an NBA player in 2014–15

6 feet 3: Stephen Curry, (2009–, 2015 NBA Most Valuable Player)

5 feet 9: average height of an American man

5 feet 3: Tyrone "Muggsy" Bogues (1987–2001, 6,726 career **assists**)

**assist:** to pass the ball to a teammate who then makes a shot

**blocked shot:** when a shot is prevented from getting to the basket by a player knocking it out of the air

8 ft

7 ft

6 ft

5 ft

4 ft

3 ft

2 ft

1 ft

0 ft

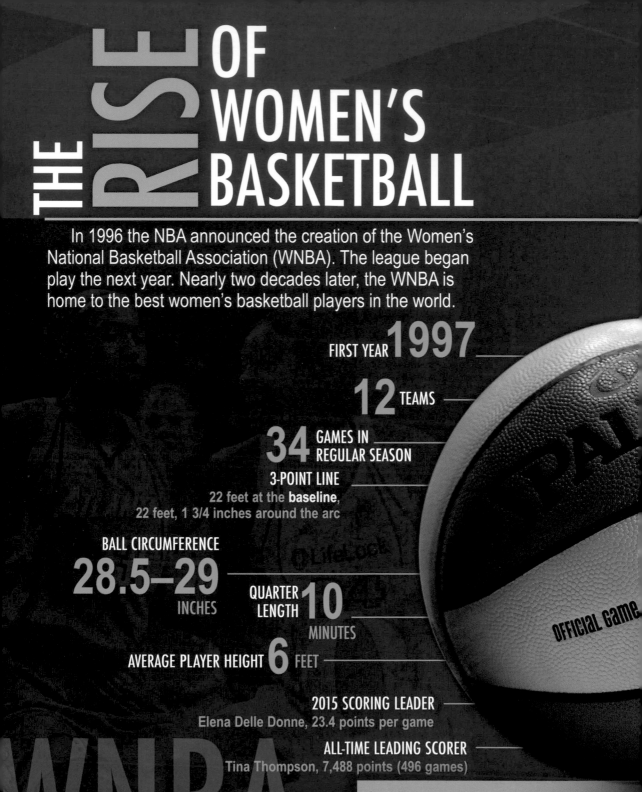

# THE RISE OF WOMEN'S BASKETBALL

In 1996 the NBA announced the creation of the Women's National Basketball Association (WNBA). The league began play the next year. Nearly two decades later, the WNBA is home to the best women's basketball players in the world.

**FIRST YEAR 1997**

**12 TEAMS**

**34 GAMES IN REGULAR SEASON**

**3-POINT LINE**
22 feet at the **baseline**,
22 feet, 1 3/4 inches around the arc

**BALL CIRCUMFERENCE**
**28.5–29 INCHES**

**QUARTER LENGTH 10 MINUTES**

**AVERAGE PLAYER HEIGHT 6 FEET**

**2015 SCORING LEADER**
Elena Delle Donne, 23.4 points per game

**ALL-TIME LEADING SCORER**
Tina Thompson, 7,488 points (496 games)

WNBA

baseline: the end line on a basketball court, running sideline to sideline behind each basket

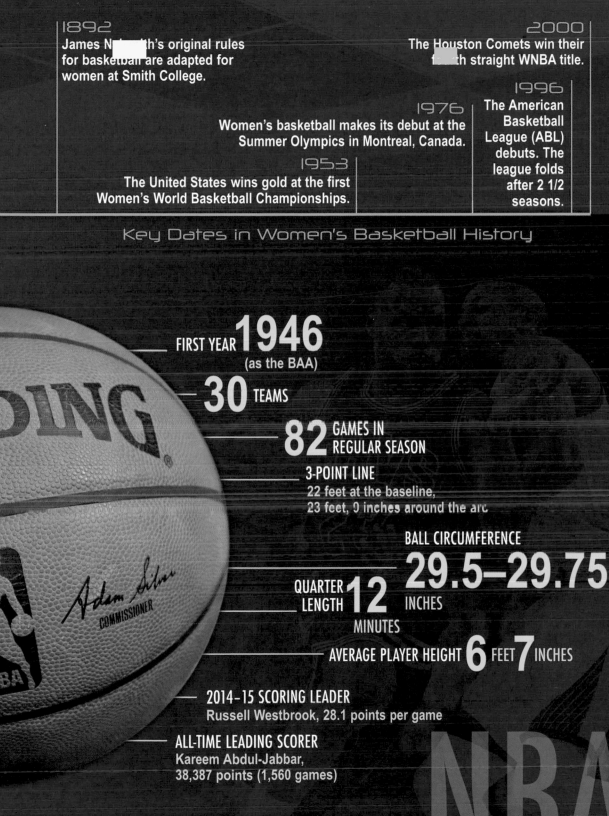

**1892**
James Naismith's original rules for basketball are adapted for women at Smith College.

**2000**
The Houston Comets win their fourth straight WNBA title.

**1996**
The American Basketball League (ABL) debuts. The league folds after 2 1/2 seasons.

**1976**
Women's basketball makes its debut at the Summer Olympics in Montreal, Canada.

**1953**
The United States wins gold at the first Women's World Basketball Championships.

## Key Dates in Women's Basketball History

FIRST YEAR **1946**
(as the BAA)

**30** TEAMS

**82** GAMES IN REGULAR SEASON

3-POINT LINE
22 feet at the baseline,
23 feet, 9 inches around the arc

BALL CIRCUMFERENCE
**29.5–29.75** INCHES

QUARTER LENGTH **12** MINUTES

AVERAGE PLAYER HEIGHT **6** FEET **7** INCHES

2014–15 SCORING LEADER
Russell Westbrook, 28.1 points per game

ALL-TIME LEADING SCORER
Kareem Abdul-Jabbar,
38,387 points (1,560 games)

NBA

# AT THE LINE

Players are awarded **free throws** after **fouls** in certain situations. These **uncontested** shots can make a huge difference in the outcome of a game.

Career free-throw shooting percentage

BEST EVER **Steve Nash, .904\***
WORST EVER **Andre Drummond, .397\*\***
2014-15 LEAGUE AVERAGE **.750**

*minimum 1,200 attempts
**minimum 500 attempts

**3.5** FEET
height of the **backboard**

## TOP PERFORMANCES

**28** most free throws made in a game, Wilt Chamberlain (1962) and Adrian Dantley (1984)

**39** most free-throw attempts in a game, Dwight Howard (2012 and 2013)

**24** most free throws made in a game without a miss, Dirk Nowitzki (2011)

**97** most free throws made in a row, Micheal Williams (3/24/93 to 11/9/93)

Points Scored in 2014-15

**17.1**%
FREE THROWS

**23.5**%
3-POINT SHOTS

**59.3**%
2-POINT SHOTS

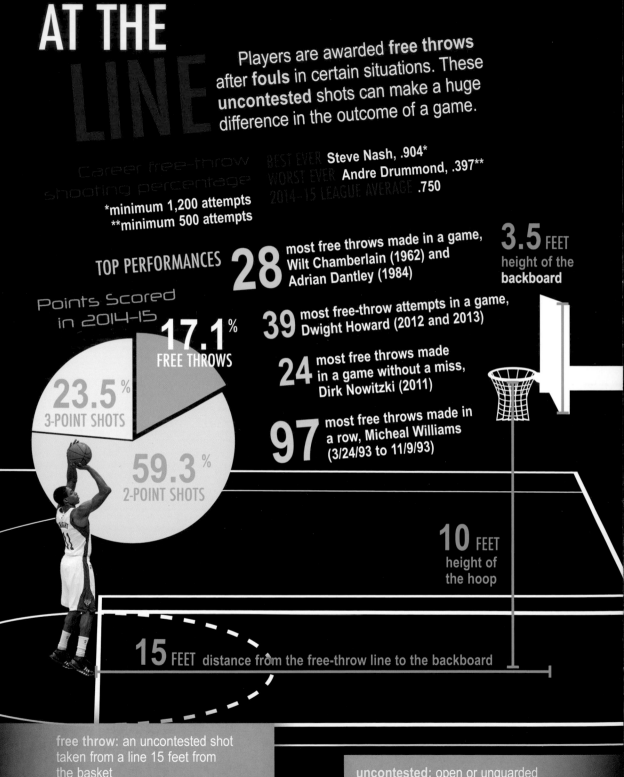

**10** FEET
height of the hoop

**15** FEET distance from the free-throw line to the backboard

free throw: an uncontested shot taken from a line 15 feet from the basket
foul: a rules violation committed against a player of the opposing team

uncontested: open or unguarded
backboard: a glass rectangle behind the hoop and net

# FROM DOWNTOWN

A 3-pointer can get a losing team back in the game quickly. Having a player who can score from way downtown—that is, a long way from the basket—when the team needs it most can be huge. The 3-point line was first used in the American Basketball League in 1961. The NBA didn't adopt it until 1979.

**19** INCHES

distance the NBA moved the line toward the hoop in 1994. The league 3-point percentage didn't change much, but attempts increased. The line was moved back to its original position in 1997.

## TOP PERFORMANCES

**286** most 3-pointers made in a season, Stephen Curry (2014–15)

**9** most 3-pointers made in a game without a miss, Latrell Sprewell (2003) and Ben Gordon (2006 and 2012)

**12** most 3-pointers made in a game, Kobe Bryant (2003) and Donyell Marshall (2005)

**13** most consecutive 3-pointers made, Brent Price (1/15/1996 to 1/19/1996) and Terry Mills (12/4/1996 to 12/7/1996)

Heat map for Stephen Curry's long-distance shooting in 2014–15

Career 3-point shooting percentage

BEST EVER **Steve Kerr, .454***
WORST EVER **Andre Miller, .217***
2014-15 LEAGUE AVERAGE **.350**

*minimum 250 attempts

MORE

PTS

FEWER

**22** FEET

**23** FEET **9** INCHES

# THE DUNK

## 1986

5-foot-7-inch Spud Webb wins the NBA dunk contest, the shortest player ever to do so.

## 1976

Julius "Dr. J" Erving takes off from the free-throw line (15 feet) to win.

## 2008

While wearing a Superman cape, Dwight Howard becomes the tallest player to ever win, at 6 feet 11 inches.

## 1988

Michael Jordan wins the contest in front of his hometown fans in Chicago.

# ARTISTS

## 2006

**Nate Robinson (only 5 feet 9 inches tall) dunks over Spud Webb to win.**

In 1976 the American Basketball Association (ABA) held a **dunk** contest. The ABA later folded but some of its teams joined the NBA. The dunk contest also survived the collapse of the ABA. The NBA has hosted a dunk contest during its All-Star weekend since 1984. It is an opportunity for the league's high-flying experts to show what they can do.

## 2011

**Blake Griffin jumps over a car (57.3 inches high) parked in the lane for the winning dunk.**

**dunk:** to jump and throw the ball down directly through the hoop

# THE BIG DIPPER GOES FOR 100

In 1962 Wilt Chamberlain was already one of the most dominant players in the game. On March 2 of that year, his Philadelphia Warriors faced the New York Knicks. That night Chamberlain did something that no NBA player has ever come close to matching—before or since. The man called "The Big Dipper" scored 100 points in one game.

| WARRIORS | FIELD GOALS MADE | FIELD GOALS ATTEMPTED | FREE THROWS MADE | FREE THROWS ATTEMPTED | POINTS |
|---|---|---|---|---|---|
| Arizin | 7 | 18 | 2 | 2 | 16 |
| Meschery | 7 | 12 | 2 | 2 | 16 |
| CHAMBERLAIN | 36 | 63 | 28 | 32 | 100 |
| Rodgers | 1 | 4 | 9 | 12 | 11 |
| Attles | 8 | 8 | 1 | 1 | 17 |
| Larese | 4 | 5 | 1 | 1 | 9 |
| Conlin | 0 | 4 | 0 | 0 | 0 |
| Ruklick | 0 | 1 | 0 | 2 | 0 |
| Luckenbill | 0 | 0 | 0 | 0 | 0 |
| Totals | 63 | 115 | 43 | 52 | 169 |

| SCORE BY QUARTERS | 1 | 2 | 3 | 4 | FINAL |
|---|---|---|---|---|---|
| Philadelphia | 42 | 37 | 46 | 44 | 169 |
| New York | 26 | 42 | 38 | 41 | 147 |

## OTHER HIGH-SCORING GAMES

| Player, Team, Date | Points |
|---|---|
| Michael Jordan, Chicago Bulls, 3/28/1990 | 69 |
| Wilt Chamberlain, San Francisco Warriors, 3/10/1963 | 70 |
| Elgin Baylor, Los Angeles Lakers, 11/15/1960 | 71 |
| David Robinson, San Antonio Spurs, 4/24/1994 | 71 |
| Wilt Chamberlain, San Francisco Warriors, 11/3/1962 | 72 |
| Wilt Chamberlain, Philadelphia Warriors, 1/13/1962 | 73 |
| Wilt Chamberlain, San Francisco Warriors, 11/16/1962 | 73 |
| David Thompson, Denver Nuggets, 4/9/1978 | 73 |
| Wilt Chamberlain, Philadelphia Warriors, 12/8/1961 | 78 |
| Kobe Bryant, Los Angeles Lakers, 1/22/2006 | 81 |

0    20    40    60    80 Points

**50.4** Chamberlain's per-game scoring average in 1961–62. That is still an NBA record.

**31.6** Walt Bellamy's per-game scoring average in 1961–62. He finished second in the scoring race.

**36** field goals (still an NBA record)

**63** field goal attempts (still an NBA record)

**28** OF **32** free-throw totals; at .875 it was much higher than his career percentage of .511

**PHILADELPHIA WARRIORS 169, NEW YORK KNICKS 147**
3/2/1962, at Hershey, Pennsylvania
Attendance: **4,124**

Most points in a game by two teams combined

**370** Detroit (186) at Denver (184) in triple overtime, 12/13/1983

**337** San Antonio (171) at Milwaukee (166) in triple overtime, 3/6/1982

**320** Golden State (162) at Denver (158), 11/2/1990

**field goal:** a shot that is not a free throw

# THE BEST OF THE BEST

## CELTICS vs. LAKERS

The Boston Celtics and the Los Angeles Lakers are two of the NBA's most storied franchises. But who comes out on top? Compare their all-time accomplishments, from their humble beginnings through the 2014–15 season.

| 1946–47 | First season | 1947–48 |
| --- | --- | --- |
| | | (as the NBL's Minneapolis Lakers) |
| 3,173 | Wins | 3,218 |
| 2,223 | Losses | 2,069 |
| 52 | Playoff appearances | 60 |
| 17 | Championships | 16 |
| 27 | Hall of Famers | 21 |

# 1995–96
# CHICAGO BULLS

**GAME 75**

The Bulls lose their first home game all season; they finish 39–2 at home.

The Celtics and Lakers might be the two greatest franchises of all time. But the Chicago Bulls put together the most amazing single season in NBA history. The Bulls went 72–10 during the 1995–96 season. No NBA team has won more games in one year. The Bulls also lost only three games in four playoff series en route to winning the NBA title.

**GAME 54**

The Bulls lose their third game in February, their most in any month.

**GAMES 27–44**

The Bulls win 18 games in a row, including every game in January 1996.

## 2
All-Star players (Michael Jordan and Scottie Pippen)

## 105.2
points per game (No. 1 in the NBA)

## 92.9
points allowed per game (No. 3 in the NBA)

## 3
future Hall of Famers on the team (Jordan, Pippen, and Dennis Rodman)

WINS

# TOP PERFORMERS

Calendar Month

| | 1 | 2 | 3 | 4 | 5 | 6 |
|---|---|---|---|---|---|---|
| 7 | 8 | 9 | 10 | 11 | 12 | 13 |
| 14 | 15 | 16 | 17 | 18 | 19 | 20 |
| 21 | 22 | 23 | 24 | 25 | 26 | 27 |
| 28 | 29 | 30 | 31 | 1 | 2 | 3 |

Calendar Month

| 4 | 5 | 6 | 7 | 8 | | |
|---|---|---|---|---|---|---|

## 57,446 MINUTES

time Kareem Abdul-Jabbar played in his career. That's 39 days, 21 hours, and 26 minutes of basketball!

## 2,973

number of 3-pointers Ray Allen made in his career. That's a combined distance of more than 13 miles, or half the distance of the Boston Marathon!

## 15,837

number of career field goals for Abdul-Jabbar. The closest active player, Kobe Bryant, would need more than 4,000 more to catch him.

## 9,787

career free throws made by longtime Utah Jazz star Karl Malone. That's nearly 28 miles of free throws, enough to get across the Great Salt Lake.

# Double-Doubles and Beyond

If a player reaches double figures in two categories in a game (such as 10 or more points and assists), that player is said to have recorded a double-double. If a player reaches double figures in three categories (usually points, rebounds, and assists), that's a triple-double. It's a good indicator of players with a variety of skills. Here are some of the best at it.

**181** most career triple-doubles, Oscar Robertson. Robertson had 41 of these during the 1961–62 season, in which he averaged a triple-double for the season. Robertson averaged 30.8 points, 12.8 rebounds, and 11.4 assists per game.

**968** most career double-doubles, Wilt Chamberlain

**4** number of players to have recorded a quadruple-double; Nate Thurmond, Alvin Robertson, Hakeem Olajuwon (twice), and David Robinson. All four reached double figures in points, rebounds, and assists. Thurmond, Olajuwon, and Robinson also reached double figures in blocked shots; Robertson did it in steals.

**0** number of players to have ever recorded a quintuple-double, though WNBA star Tamika Catchings did it in high school

# Glossary

**assist (uh-SISST)**—to pass the ball to a teammate who then makes a shot

**backboard (BAK-bord)**—a glass rectangle behind the hoop and net

**baseline (BAYSS-line)**—the end line on a basketball court, running sideline to sideline behind each basket

**blocked shot (BLOKD SHOT)**—when a shot is prevented from getting to the basket by a player knocking it out of the air

**court (KORT)**—the playing surface for basketball

**dunk (DUHNGK)**—to jump and throw the ball down directly through the hoop

**field goal (FEELD GOHL)**—a shot that is not a free throw

**foul (FOUL)**—a rules violation committed against a player of the opposing team

**free throw (FREE THROH)**—an uncontested shot taken from a line 15 feet from the basket

**key (KEE)**—the painted area under the basket; also known as the "lane"

**overtime (OH-vur-time)**—an extra period played to determine a winner if regulation ends in a tie

**playoffs (PLAY-ofss)**—the tournament held after the regular season to crown the NBA champions

**regulation (reg-yuh-LAY-shuhn)**—the scheduled time period of a basketball game; in the NBA it lasts 48 minutes

**uncontested (uhn-kuhn-TEST-id)**—open or unguarded

# Read More

**Adamson, Thomas K.** *Basketball: The Math of the Game.* Kids Sports Math. Mankato, Minn.: Capstone Press, 2012.

**Slade, Suzanne.** *The Technology of Basketball.* High–Tech Sports. North Mankato, Minn.: Capstone Press, 2013.

# Critical Thinking Using the Common Core

1. On pages 14 and 15 you learned about the history of the shot clock in the NBA. Why do you think NBA owners wanted to increase scoring in their games? (Integration of Knowledge and Ideas)

2. Nobody has come close to matching Wilt Chamberlain's 100-point game. But on that night Chamberlain also took more shots than any player has ever taken in an NBA game. His teammates wanted him to reach 100 points, so they passed him the ball more often. Does that make Chamberlain's feat less impressive in your opinion? Why or why not? (Key Ideas and Details)

# Internet Sites

FactHound offers a safe, fun way to find Internet sites related to this book. All of the sites on FactHound have been researched by our staff.

Visit *www.facthound.com*

Type in this code: 9781491490587

Check out projects, games and lots more at
**www.capstonekids.com**

Graphic Library is published by Capstone Press,
1710 Roe Crest Drive, North Mankato, Minnesota 56003
www.capstonepub.com

Library of Congress Cataloging-in-Publication Data

Enz, Tammy.
  Super cool mechanical activities with Max Axiom / by Tammy Enz.
     pages cm.—(Graphic library. Max Axiom science and engineering
activities)
  Audience: Ages 8–14.
  Audience: Grade 4 to 6.
  Summary   uper Scientist, Max Axiom, presents step-by-step
photo-illustrated instructions for building a variety of machines"—
Provided by publisher.
  Includes bibliographical references and index.
  ISBN 978-1-4914-2080-5 (library binding)
  ISBN 978-1-4914-2284-7 (paperback)
  ISBN 978-1-4914-2298-4 (eBook PDF)
1. Mechanical engineering—Juvenile literature. 2. Machinery—Comic
books, strips, etc. 3. Graphic novels. I. Title.
  TJ147.E589 2015
  621—dc23                                    2014027881

Editor
Christopher L. Harbo

Project Creation
Sarah Schuette and Marcy Morin

Art Director
Nathan Gassman

Photographs by Capstone Studio:
Karon Dubke

Designer
Tracy McCabe

Production Specialist
Katy LaVigne

Cover Illustration
Marcelo Baez

# Table of Contents

SUPER COOL MACHINES........... 4

HOVERCRAFT............................ 6

PULLEY SYSTEM........................ 8

DIVING SUBMARINE................ 10

PENDULUM PAINTER .............. 12

PUMP DRILL............................ 14

TREBUCHET............................. 16

HYDRO-POWERED WINCH ...... 20

HYDRAULIC ARM .................... 24

ELECTRIC FAN MOTOR........... 26

GLOSSARY ............................... 28

READ MORE............................. 31

INTERNET SITES...................... 31

INDEX...................................... 32

Whoa! I have to stop and take a look at these turbines.

They look like mechanical trees in a huge alien forest.

But these massive machines are actually simple contraptions.

They turn wind—the product of cool air rushing in to replace rising hot air—into usable energy.

A wind turbine's inner workings may seem like a mystery.

But a closer look shows how spinning blades turn a generator to make electricity.

BLADES

GENERATOR

turbine—an engine powered by steam or gas; the steam or gas moves through the blades of a fanlike device and makes it turn

# HOVERCRAFT

Wind turbines aren't the only air-powered machines. This peppy little hovercraft glides across your floor on a cushion of moving air.

## YOU'LL NEED

hot glue gun

push-top water bottle cap

old CD

large balloon

## SAFETY FIRST

Ask an adult for permission to use a hot glue gun before starting this project.

# PLAN OF ACTION

1. Place a bead of hot glue along the bottom edge of the bottle cap. Quickly center the cap over the hole in the CD. Hold it in place for about 15 seconds. Push the top of the cap down to close it.

2. Blow up the balloon and pinch the neck closed to seal in the air. Carefully stretch the mouth of the balloon over the top of the bottle cap.

3. Place the hovercraft on a smooth surface and pull up on the bottle cap's push top to open it. Release the neck of the balloon with a gentle push.

4. Watch the hovercraft sail across the surface on a cushion of air.

## AXIOM ALTERNATIVE

Attach the hovercraft *horizontally* to the back of a small car or set of wheels. See if the machine's backward thrust can push the car forward. Also try cutting fins into a paper plate and using it in place of the CD. Does this change the hover action?

**horizontal**—flat and parallel to the ground

# PULLEY SYSTEM

A pulley is a simple machine made of a wheel turned by a rope or a belt. A pulley system helps lift and move objects. Pulleys change the direction and location of pulling or lifting forces. Try out this system to lift and lower an action figure from across the room.

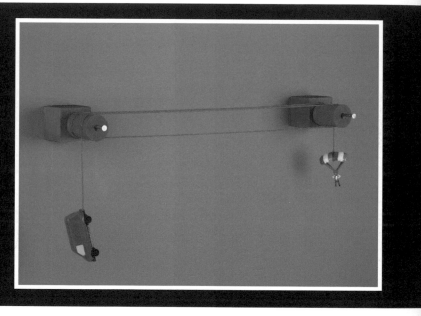

## YOU'LL NEED

pencil

4 removable adhesive tabs*

2 2-inch x 2-inch x ¾-inch (5-cm x 5-cm x 2-cm) wood blocks

2 empty thread spools

2 3½-inch- (9-cm-) long nails

hammer

ball of string

scissors

2 small toys

*typically found with adhesive wall hooks

# PLAN OF ACTION

1. Ask an adult to help you find an empty wall you can use. Mark two dots at the same height at opposite ends of the wall. At each mark, stick two adhesive tabs with a 1-inch (2.5-cm) gap between them.

2. Place a nail through the center of each spool.

3. Hammer a spool into the center of each of the wooden blocks. Make sure the spools can spin freely.

4. Stick the blocks to adhesive tabs on both ends of the wall.

5. Place the ball of string on the ground under one of the spools. Unwind the string and guide it over the top of this spool. Then carefully pull it to and over the top of the other spool.

6. Pull the string under the second spool and guide it back to and around the first spool. Then pull it back to and over the top of the second spool once again.

7. Let the string hang down to the ground from the second spool. Snip this end of the string off about halfway up the wall.

8. Tie a small toy to each end of the string. Pulling or releasing the figure at either end will do the opposite to the other figure.

## ⚡ AXIOM ALTERNATIVE

*This pulley system has more potential than just lifting objects. See if you can use it to send notes back and forth across the room.*

**adhesive** —a substance, such as glue, that makes things stick together

# DIVING SUBMARINE

Submarines use pumps to fill large tanks, called ballasts, with either air or water. Air-filled tanks make the sub more **buoyant** and allow it to float to the surface. When the pumps fill the ballasts with water, the sub becomes less buoyant and sinks below the waves. Make your own submarine to see this action at work.

## YOU'LL NEED

plastic drink bottle with a push-top cap

utility knife

2 1-inch- (2.5-cm-) diameter washers

4-foot- (120-cm-) long vinyl hose with an outside dimension of 5/8 inch (16 mm) and an inside dimension of 1/2 inch (13 mm)

hot glue gun

tub or pool of water

## SAFETY FIRST

Ask an adult for permission to use a utility knife and hot glue gun before starting this project.

# PLAN OF ACTION

1. Use the utility knife to carefully cut two holes on one side of the bottle. The holes should be about the size of a pencil eraser and about 3 inches (7.5 cm) apart.

2. Glue a washer over each of these holes. The washer holes should line up with the bottle's holes.

3. With the bottle cap opened, slide the hose around its tip. Make sure the hose fits tightly. Use hot glue to seal the hose in place if needed.

4. Put the submarine in a tub or pool of water with the hose above the water. Watch the submarine sink as water enters its holes. Make it sink faster by gently sucking on the hose.

5. When the submarine is under water, blow into the hose to make it rise to the water's surface.

## ⚡ AXIOM ALTERNATIVE

*Try using a flexible hose and changing the position of the air/water release holes. See if the pump action can move the submarine forward or backward.*

**buoyant**—able to keep afloat

**dimension**—an object's measurement or size; an object's dimensions are length, width, and height

# PENDULUM PAINTER

A pendulum provides a perfect example of **potential energy** and **kinetic energy** in action. When an object on the end of a string swings upward, it gains potential energy. Gravity then pulls the object downward to change the potential energy to kinetic energy. When the pendulum swings upward again, its energy changes back to potential energy. And so the process repeats. Try using pendulum power to paint some super cool designs.

## YOU'LL NEED

3 5/16-inch- (8-mm-) diameter by 4-foot- (122-cm-) long wooden dowels

4-foot- (122-cm-) long piece of string

scissors

clean travel size lotion bottle with lid

large sewing needle

2 large paper clips

30-inch- (76-cm-) long piece of string

washable poster paint

water

coffee stir stick

large sheets of paper

# PLAN OF ACTION

1. Arrange the dowels to form a tripod with legs about 2 feet (0.6 m) apart. Let the tops of the dowels cross each other and overlap by about 4 inches (10 cm).

2. Wrap the 4-foot (1.2-m) string tightly around and under the crossing dowels. Continue wrapping until the tripod is tightly bound and its legs stay in position. Tie off the ends of the string.

3. Cut off the bottom of the lotion bottle with a scissors.

4. Use the needle to poke two holes on opposite sides of the bottle about 1/2 inch (1 cm) from the open end.

**potential energy**—the stored energy of an object that is raised, stretched, or squeezed

**kinetic energy**—the energy of a moving object

*continued*

5. Straighten the middle twist in each of the paper clips. Both paper clips will now have bends on each end.

6. Clip one end of each paper clip through a hole in the lotion bottle.

7. Tie a 1-inch (2.5-cm) loop in one end of the 30-inch (76-cm) piece of string. Tie the other end around the tripod top, leaving the loop hanging down.

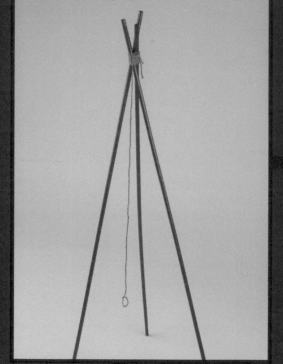

8. Clip the paper clip hooks to the loop.

9. With the lid closed, fill the lotion bottle about one-third full with poster paint. Fill another third of the bottle with water. Use the stir stick to mix the paint.

10. Position a large sheet of paper under the painter. Carefully open the cap. Swing and twirl the bottle to watch the pendulum paint a design on the paper.

## AXIOM ALTERNATIVE

*Try attaching a second string and bottle with a different color paint. Swing the bottles at the same time to create an even more colorful painting. Try using different lengths of string to see how the design changes.*

# PUMP DRILL

A pump drill is an ancient tool still used today. It uses **momentum** created by the spinning motion of a disc placed on a shaft to create a drilling motion. See this amazing pump drill in action for yourself!

## YOU'LL NEED

¾-inch (19-mm) x 18-inch (46-cm) wooden dowel

wood saw

2-inch (5-cm) nail

hammer

wire snips

5½-inch x 1½-inch x ¾-inch (14-cm x 4-cm x 2-cm) block of wood

drill

⅞-inch (22-mm) drill bit

⅛-inch (3-mm) drill bit

30-inch- (76-cm-) long piece of string

large plastic coffee can lid

utility knife

electrical tape

piece of scrap wood

## SAFETY FIRST

Ask an adult for help when asked to use a drill, saw, or utility knife for this project.

momentum—the amount of motion an object carries

*continued*

# PLAN OF ACTION

1. Cut a 1/2-inch (2-cm) deep slit in one end of the dowel with the saw.

2. Pound the nail into the center of the other end of the dowel with the hammer. Leave about 1 inch (3 cm) of the nail sticking out. Snip off the head of the nail with the wire snips.

3. Drill a hole into the center of the small piece of wood with the 7/8-inch (22-mm) drill bit.

5. Thread one end of the string through one of the small holes. Knot the end. Repeat this step with the other end of the string and the second small hole. Make sure the knots are large enough so they do not slip through the holes.

4. Drill two small holes in the piece of wood with the 1/8-inch (3-mm) drill bit. Each hole should be centered about 1/2 inch (2 cm) from the ends of the wood.

6. Slide the dowel through the large hole. Insert the string through the slit in the dowel.

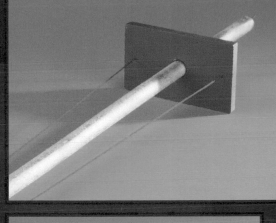

7. Cut a hole through the center of the coffee can lid with the utility knife. Make the hole just large enough so the dowel fits snugly through it.

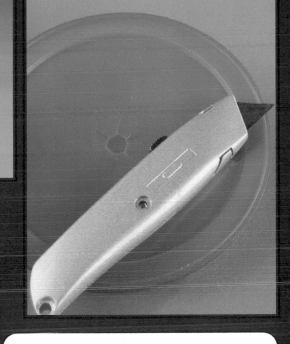

8. Slide the lid up the dowel so that it rests just below the piece of wood hanging on the string. Tape the lid in place.

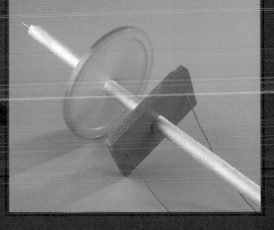

9. Wrap the string around the dowel a few times by turning the piece of wood. Position the pump drill's nail on a piece of scrap wood. Start drilling by pushing the pump drill's wood handle downward. Allow momentum to pull the handle back up before pushing it down again. This momentum will cause the dowel to spin and the nail to drill a hole.

## ⚡ AXIOM ALTERNATIVE

*Experiment with different drill bits. Try using a screw instead of a nail for better precision or for drilling a larger hole.*

# TREBUCHET

A trebuchet was a weapon used in the Middle Ages. This mechanical throwing device uses gravity's pull on a **counterweight** to fling an object. In a few simple steps, your trebuchet will fling marbles across the room.

## YOU'LL NEED

8 large wooden craft sticks

ruler

hot glue gun

2 wooden chopsticks

rubber band

plastic drink bottle cap

drill

1/8-inch (3-mm) drill bit

masking tape

4 1-inch- (2.5-cm-) diameter washers

marble

## SAFETY FIRST

Ask an adult for permission to use a hot glue gun and drill before starting this project.

# PLAN OF ACTION

1. Lay three craft sticks out to form a triangle. Overlap their ends so that the ends are **flush** at two points of the triangle. At the third point, they should overlap each other by 1 inch (3 cm). Glue the sticks in this position.

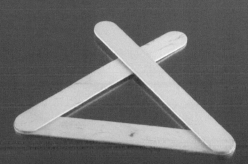

2. Repeat step 1 with three more sticks.

3. Lay the remaining two sticks parallel to each other and about 5 inches (13 cm) apart. Straddle the sticks with the flush sides of the upright triangles, placing them about 4 inches (10 cm) apart. Glue them in place.

4. Form a cross with the chopsticks. Wind the rubber band tightly around the cross to hold the pieces together.

counterweight—a weight that balances a load

flush—exactly even

19

5. Drill a hole in the side of the plastic cap. Slide one end of one chopstick into it. Secure with glue.

6. On the other end of the chopstick with the cap, wrap several layers of masking tape. Slide the washers over the masking tape, making sure they fit very snugly.

7. Set the arms of the cross over the triangle supports. Adjust the rubber band so the washers can swing freely below the crossbar.

8. Pull the cap back and place a marble in it. Release the lid to fling the marble.

⚡ AXIOM ALTERNATIVE

*Some trebuchets used a sling instead of a fixed basket. Try replacing the cap with a sling for flinging the marble.*

# HYDRO-POWERED WINCH

Moving water is a powerful force. Falling water can turn a wheel to generate electricity, run a sawmill, or grind grain. With just a few household supplies, you can build a water wheel winch.

## YOU'LL NEED

empty 2-liter bottle

ruler

pencil

utility knife

2 small binder clips

2 thin plastic container lids

scissors

chopstick

12-inch (30-cm) piece of string

tape

small toy

pitcher

water

## SAFETY FIRST

Ask an adult for help when asked to use a utility knife for this project.

continued

1. Measure 7 inches (18 cm) up from the bottom of the 2-liter bottle. Mark a line all around the bottle at this height. Carefully cut along this line with the utility knife to remove the top of the bottle.

2. Set the bottle top upside down inside the bottom of the bottle. Clip the binder clips opposite from each other along the edge of the bottle top. Flip the inside handles of the binder clips down.

3. Measure and cut two 2¾-inch x 3-inch (70-mm x 76-mm) rectangles from the centers of the plastic lids.

4. Fold one piece of plastic in half along the short dimension.

5. Measure and mark lines every ½ inch (13 mm) along the folded edge.

6. Use a scissors to cut short slits at each mark.

7. Repeat steps 4 through 6 with the other plastic piece.

8. Unfold the rectangles and lay them back-to-back so their slits line up. Weave the chopstick through the slits in both pieces of plastic to hold them together. Spread the four plastic flaps apart to create a water wheel.

9. Slide the chopstick ends through the handles on the binder clips.

10. Tie and tape the string to the longer side of the chopstick. Tie the toy to the end of the string.

11. Gently pour water from the pitcher onto the center of one of the paddles to turn the winch. As the winch turns it will lift the toy.

## AXIOM ALTERNATIVE

*Apply moving air to the paddles with a hair dryer. You'll convert the winch from hydropower to wind power. Which has more lifting power, wind or water?*

# HYDRAULIC ARM

Heavy machinery and many mechanical devices use hydraulic power. Hydraulics use pressurized fluid to lift, push, pull, and dig. Experiment with the power of hydraulics with a simple hydraulic digging arm project.

## YOU'LL NEED

6 large wooden craft sticks

ruler

hot glue gun

pencil

drill

1/8-inch (3-mm) drill bit

2 brass fasteners

plastic fork

2 syringes

heavy duty shears

12-inch- (30-cm-) long plastic hose with a 1/8-inch (3-mm) inside diameter

small binder clip

## SAFETY FIRST

Ask an adult for permission to use a hot glue gun and drill before starting this project.

# PLAN OF ACTION

1. Place two craft sticks parallel to each other. Their outside edges should be about 6 inches (15 cm) apart.

2. Place a drop of hot glue on the center of each stick. Place another stick across the first two to form a letter H. Hold it to the hot glue for about 15 seconds.

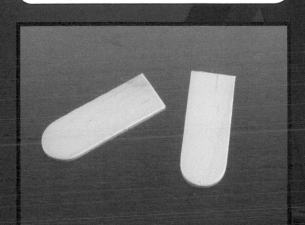

3. Measure and mark a line 2 inches (5 cm) from each end of another stick. Use the shears to cut along each of these lines. Discard the center portion.

4. On one of the 2-inch (5-cm) pieces, measure and mark a dot ¼-inch (6-mm) down from the center of the rounded end. Drill a hole at this dot.

5. Repeat step 4 with the remaining 2-inch (5-cm) piece.

7. Glue one edge of the other 2-inch (5-cm) piece to the center of the flat side of another craft stick. Line up their rounded ends

6. Glue the cut end of one of the 2-inch (5-cm) pieces to the center of the H created in step 2. The piece should stand straight up.

*continued*

8. On the remaining stick, measure and mark a dot 1/4 inch (6 mm) from the center of each rounded end. Drill holes at each dot.

9. Line up the holes in the long stick with the holes in each of the 2-inch (5-cm) pieces. Connect the pieces with the brass fasteners.

10. Use the shears to cut the handle off the fork and discard it. Glue the fork head, tines down, to the top of the digging arm. The fork should extend off the end of the arm.

11. Insert each of the syringe tips into either end of the hose. Remove one of the syringe's plungers. Close the other syringe's plunger.

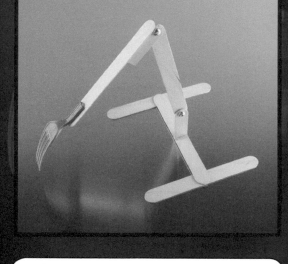

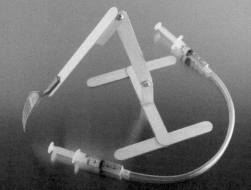

12. With help from a friend, fill the empty plunger with water, pulling the other plunger to fill the hose and syringe. Replace the first plunger. Adjust the syringes so that as one opens, the other closes.

13. Glue the end of one of the plungers to the bottom of the digging arm.

14. Secure the hose to the upright stick with the binder clip. Adjust its location so the arm swings easily up and down when the plunger on the unsecured syringe is pushed or pulled.

## AXIOM ALTERNATIVE

*For better digging action, try adding a bending joint where the fork attaches to the machine. You can also replace the fork with a spoon for lifting objects, or try adding a paintbrush for painting a design.*

# ELECTRIC FAN MOTOR

Most motors hide inside the machines they run. But if you could peel back the layers, you'd see an amazingly simple concept at work. Motors use the attracting and repelling properties of magnets to their advantage. An electric current in a loop of wire creates a magnetic field that spins when it is near a magnet. Witness this concept in action by building your own motor-powered fan.

## YOU'LL NEED

5 feet (1.5 m) of enamel-coated magnet wire

broom

sandpaper

1½-inch (4-cm) square of paper

scissors

hot glue gun

sewing needle

2 large metal paper clips

needle-nosed pliers

6-inch- (15-cm-) long 2 x 4 board

heavy duty stapler

3 1-inch- (2.5-cm) diameter circular magnets

2 5-inch- (13-cm-) long plastic coated electrical wires

wire-stripping tool

2 small alligator clips

electrical tape

AA battery

## SAFETY FIRST

Ask an adult for permission to use a hot glue gun before starting this project.

continued

# PLAN OF ACTION

2. Use the sandpaper to sand off all the enamel on one of the 2-inch (5-cm) ends. Sand only one side of the enamel off the other 2-inch (5-cm) end.

1. Wind the enamel-coated wire around the broom handle at least 15 times. Leave 2 inches (5 cm) loose at each end. Wrap each end twice around the coil on opposite sides to hold the coils together.

3. Cut diagonal slits almost to the center from each corner of the paper.

4. Bend the corner of every other paper flap into the center of the paper. Hot glue the corners to the center to make fan blades.

5. Use the needle to punch a hole through the center of the dried hot glue. Stick one end of the coiled wire into the hole on the back side of the fan.

6. Bend one loop of a paper clip at a 90-degree angle. Use the pliers to kink the end of this loop into a small S shape. Repeat with the other paper clip.

7. Staple the unkinked loops of the paper clips about 2½ inches (6 cm) apart near one end of the 2 x 4.

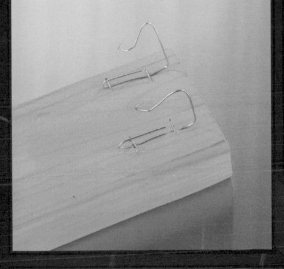

8. Place the wire coil across the paper clip supports. Stack the magnets under the coils.

10. Clip each alligator clip to one end of the stapled paper clips. Tape their other ends to opposite sides of the battery.

9. Strip about 1 inch (3 cm) of coating from each end of one of the coated wires. Attach an alligator clip to one end. Repeat with the other wire.

11. Gently flick the wire coil to start it rotating. The fan will begin turning. It can be stopped by unclipping one of the alligator clips.

## ⚡ AXIOM ALTERNATIVE

*Try replacing the battery with a hobby-size solar cell to run the motor using an alternate energy source.*

# Glossary

**adhesive** (ad-HEE-siv)—a substance, such as glue, that makes things stick together

**buoyant** (BOI-uhnt)—able to keep afloat

**counterweight** (KAUN-tuhr-wayt)—a weight that balances a load

**dimension** (duh-MEN-shuhn)—an object's measurement or size; an object's dimensions are length, width, and height

**flush** (FLUSH)—exactly even

**horizontal** (hor-uh-ZON-tuhl)—flat and parallel to the ground

**kinetic energy** (ki-NET-ik EN-ur-jee)—the energy of a moving object

**momentum** (moh-MEN-tuhm)—the amount of motion an object carries

**potential energy** (puh-TEN-shuhl EN-ur-jee)—the stored energy of an object that is raised, stretched, or squeezed

**turbine** (TUR-bine)—an engine powered by steam or gas; the steam or gas moves through the blades of a fanlike device and makes it turn

# Read More

**Enz, Tammy.** *Zoom It: Invent New Machines that Move.* Invent It. Mankato, Minn.: Capstone Press, 2012.

**Meachen Rau, Dana.** *Simple Machines.* A True Book. New York: Children's Press, 2012.

**Rissman, Rebecca.** *Simple Machines.* Real Size Science. Chicago: Capstone Heinemann Library, 2013.

# Internet Sites

FactHound offers a safe, fun way to find Internet sites related to this book. All of the sites on FactHound have been researched by our staff.

Here's all you do:

Visit *www.facthound.com*

Type in this code: 9781491420805

Check out projects, games and lots more at
**www.capstonekids.com**

#  Index

ballasts, 10
buoyancy, 10, 11

counterweights, 18, 19

electric motors, 27–29

gravity, 12, 18

hovercrafts, 6–7
hydraulics, 24–26
hydropower, 21–23

kinetic energy, 12, 13

magnets, 27, 29
momentum, 15, 17

pendulums, 12–14
potential energy, 12, 13
pulleys, 8–9
pump drills, 15–17

submarines, 10–11

trebuchets, 18–20
turbines, 4–5, 6

winches, 21–23
wind power, 4–5, 6, 23